Technology
Past and Present

Daniel Shepard

Rigby®

A Harcourt Achieve Imprint

www.Rigby.com
1-800-531-5015

Do you use a computer?
Does someone you know
have a cell phone?
Now imagine a world
without these things.
Let's see how some other things
have changed over the last fifty years.

Fifty years ago, a television's picture was only in black and white. The televisions were also very big, but their pictures were small.

What do you think your favorite show would look like on an old television?

Today televisions can be tiny or huge. Some can even hang on the wall! The pictures are easier to see, and they are in color.

In the past, people listened to music on **records**.
The records would spin on a record player.
One side of the record could hold only five or six songs.
Then you had to turn it over to play the other side.

How do *you* listen to your favorite songs?

Today there are many different ways to listen to music. Music players are very small and they are easy to carry. Some of them can even hold more than 1,000 songs!

Can you guess what this is?

It's an old computer.
There were no **personal computers**
until the 1980s.

What do you think this computer
was used for?

Today computers are smaller
and much more powerful.
You can use them to send messages,
to do work, or even to play games.

Every old telephone had a cord that plugged into the wall. You also had to use a round **dial** to call someone's number.

Sometimes you had to tell an **operator** what number to call for you.

Today phones can go anywhere
people can go.
With a push of a button, you can call
people around the world.

This is what airplanes looked like
many years ago.
They were much smaller and slower
than today's airplanes.

Today people fly in big, powerful jets. These jets can go 400 miles an hour or even faster!

Color televisions, small computers, and fast jets were all **invented** in the past fifty years.

What do *you* think the **future** will bring us?
Imagine, and you can make it happen!

Glossary

dial disc with numbers that can be turned around

future the days to come

invented made something never made before

operator someone who helps you make a telephone call

personal computers computers owned and used by one person at a time

present today

records large, round, plastic discs that store music

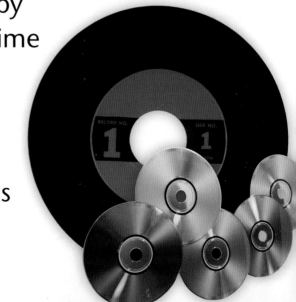